Salt and Light

America's Greatest Need

Alton Lynn Cooper

ISBN 979-8-89043-514-9 (paperback)
ISBN 979-8-89043-515-6 (digital)

Christian Faith Publishing
832 Park Avenue
Meadville, PA 16335
www.christianfaithpublishing.com

All scripture references in this book are taken from the King James Version (KJV) of God's Holy Word.

Printed in the United States of America

Contents

Foreword

Dr. Alton Lynn Cooper has served the Lord as a leader of the largest deaf ministry in the state of Michigan for many years. Upon retirement from the pastorate of that ministry, God lead him into the writing ministry, and now he has written over twenty books from children's to devotional, with all being published by well-known and established publishing houses.

I have personally known Dr. Cooper for over twenty-five years and have found him to be an honest, steadfast, godly servant of the Lord. He served under me for many years, and I could always count on him to do all that was expected and needed to advance the cause of Christ. I was impressed with his ministry skills, and I am equally impressed with his writing skills.

I would highly recommend and endorse him for his ability to speak, teach, and encourage any assembly that he is called to address. Dr. Cooper is not only accomplished in his field but is also a godly role model in his character and people skills.

Dr. Daryl L. Franzel
President, Alabama Baptist Seminary

Preface

When the question is asked what the most urgent need in our nation is, we receive a wide spectrum of responses, depending on the current circumstances swirling around us and what the most recent crises are. Individuals tend to answer this question based on their own set of circumstances and the most pressing issues affecting them at the time. Many of us tend to react to current events based on how they affect us personally in our day-to-day lives. It is our desire to live in peace, having enough of this world's creature comforts to bring joy and contentment our way.

When tragedies occur, we react to them and then quickly return to our own pursuits if the disaster happens to someone else. This is a sad pronouncement on the human race, but a true one nonetheless. Many individuals today are self-focused, primarily concerned about their own needs being met and those close to them. This is not to say that when disasters strike, such as tornadoes or hurricanes, organizations and other individuals don't rush in to help. That is a good thing. Having a heart to help others in their time of need lifts not only them up but also brings joy to us.

Our nation is in trouble today, heading toward some serious times ahead if current situations continue as they are. Some would answer the question of America's most urgent need by blaming the present difficulties on those currently holding office at the local and national levels. They do have a significant impact on the direction we're headed, but they are not the ones to blame for our failures as a society. So where does the responsibility lie for the well-being of our nation and our future?

Salt and Light is written to answer this question as America stands at a critical crossroad in our nation's history. We have strayed from God and His presence in the founding principles that have sustained us for over two hundred years. Our society today is becoming more secular, turning its back on the one who can bless our land and heal it from its sickness. Yes, America is a sin-sick nation in urgent need of care. I pray this book will speak to your heart and put within it the desire to do your part in saving the land we love.

> *Ye are the salt of the earth: but if the salt have lost his savour, wherewith shall it be salted? it is thenceforth good for nothing, but to be cast out, and to be trodden under foot of men. Ye are the light of the world. A city that is set on an hill cannot be hid. Neither do men light a candle, and put it under a bushel, but on a candlestick; and it giveth light unto all that are in the house. Let your light so shine before men, that they may see your good works, and glorify your Father which is in heaven. (Matthew 5:13–16)*

A Nation Divided

Recent polling reflects just how much our nation is divided. Political polarization is at an all-time high. It is true that we have historically had differing views concerning a myriad of directions for our country, but those have typically been in the areas of the economy, taxation, employment, and opportunities for the lower and middle classes to advance in their quality of life. There have always been dinner table discussions concerning which political party is more interested in helping the little guy and who is for big business and Wall Street. These are concerns focused on economic issues versus those of moral consideration and biblical values.

As our nation has become more secular, biblical values are not held in high esteem, and those promoting them have gained the ire of many in the political realm. This has been evidenced in the attacks on candidates who attend a house of worship and the fears expressed that their biblical views will affect how they respond to certain issues if elected. As a result, many individuals seeking elective office strive to separate their personal and public lives by operating in a secular way while serving in the office versus adhering to biblical values taught in their churches. This has been an issue recently between the Catholic Church and those currently elected to higher office concerning their position on the matter of abortion.

Conservative versus liberal views on how society functions are indeed areas of division, but the greater issues of separation are those between secular and biblical positions in today's society. America was founded on Christian values revealed in the Holy Word of God. Many have sought to deny this and change our history by defaming the Founding Fathers, ignoring their biblical beliefs and the words they spoke concerning God's influence on the constitution and the direction of our nation. As a result of these two very opposite positions, our nation is heavily divided over the issues of abortion, same-sex marriage, and more recently, gender identity. Race has also become a dividing point in our modern-day society. If a person uses a certain phrase while expressing their viewpoint on a given topic, they are often labeled as racist or worse.

Many attempt to insert division based on an individual's faith, political view, or national origin. Recently, parents became aware of the indoctrinating teaching of critical race theory in their children's classrooms as a result of distance learning because of the COVID-19 pandemic. This teaching creates a division between the races and weakens inclusion and respect for others. Dr. Martin Luther King Jr. said it right: "I have a dream that my four little children will one day live in a nation where they will not be judged by the color of their skin but by the content of their character." God's Word teaches us to love others and respect them as we would have them love and respect us. Sadly, many seek to sow discord, bringing about division and discontent for their own purposes.

There are loud voices today calling for tolerance when their true desire is for everyone else to go along with their positions, not speak out against them. Respecting another individual's views and entering into a healthy debate while remaining open-minded have become a thing of the past. This is evidenced in the silencing of certain speakers by shouting them down, whether it is in a public hearing or on many of the nation's college campuses. Student groups in some of our higher learning institutions have resorted to violence to prevent certain speakers from being allowed to express their views on current affairs. Polarization occurs when an individual completely shuts out other voices and the positions they represent. A nation divided is weakened within, leaving itself prey to outside enemies that seek to destroy it. The inability of a nation's citizens to find common ground is, indeed, dangerous and can usher in chaos and destruction.

Jesus healed an individual who had been possessed by a devil in Matthew 12:22. The Pharisees accused Him of healing the person with Satan's power. Jesus's response is applicable to our nation's division today.

> *And Jesus knew their thoughts, and said unto them, Every kingdom divided against itself is brought to desolation; and every city or house divided against itself shall not stand: (Matthew 12:25)*

The Pharisees' opposition was based on their jealousy and their rigid religious positions. They should have praised God for setting the person free from the demons that tormented him. However, their minds were completely closed to the work of God because of their malice toward Jesus. Jesus's response was direct. How can Satan cast out Satan? In effect, he would be destroying himself. Satan is smart enough not to attack his own kingdom by fighting against those serving him. That would be very unwise indeed. That is also true for our nation. How can we, as citizens, set out to destroy our fellow citizens without destroying the nation itself?

Our greatest challenge today is one of a spiritual nature.

> *For we wrestle not against flesh and blood, but against principalities, against powers, against the rulers of the darkness of this world, against spiritual wickedness in high places. (Ephesians 6:12)*

Our true battle is not politics or interpersonal differences from a societal standpoint. We are fighting a battle between light and darkness. The battle started long ago in eternity past when Lucifer rose in opposition to the one Who created him. He completely rejected God's authority, wanting to establish his own kingdom. There are forces at work in our nation today that reject the Founding Fathers and the documents that have sustained our country throughout its history. They reject the words in our pledge of allegiance. "One nation under God, indivisible, with liberty and justice for all."

In the past few years, we have watched our cities burn, our police officers assaulted and murdered, and our nation's peace taken from it by roving bands of lawbreakers. They tear down statues, desiring to destroy the memory of past heroes who fought and died for our freedom. What is America's greatest need today? What is this world's greatest need today? It is not for some well-spoken politician to arise or for any one group of governmental leaders to come on the scene. It is a return in obedience to the God Who created us and to His Holy Word.

America is in desperate need of spiritual healing. We are a nation in peril. Without God's blessing upon our country, we will continue to decline and perhaps one day cease to exist as a nation. Even though the hour is late, there is hope! I don't say these things to discourage but to encourage you. Before any problem can be solved, we must acknowledge its existence. I pray that the message in this book will open hearts and minds to what is truly needed to unite our nation once again and bring God's blessings upon it.

The Allure of Things / Materialism

Before we can understand what is needed to cure our nation of its sickness, we must clearly define what the elements of that sickness are. As previously stated, America's greatest need is not one concerning the current state of our politics but one of spiritual decline. What in this world has gotten the attention of God's children? Are we busy with our Father's work, or are we busy seeking this world's treasures? God promised throughout His Word to bless those who walk in obedience to Him and to judge and hold accountable those who reject His leadership. God never changes. He is the same yesterday, today, and forever. His promises are still the same, and His desire to bless His children on this earth is as real for us today as it was for those who have gone before us.

> *For the eyes of the LORD run to and fro throughout the whole earth, to show himself strong in the behalf of them whose heart is perfect toward Him. (2 Chronicles 16:9a)*

God has not changed. It is the people of the world who have changed. When the Antichrist comes on the scene, he will deceive many by promising peace and prosperity. These are two of the most important topics on people's minds today. Certainly, there is nothing wrong with wanting peace and prosperity, but to what extent will we go to possess them? Satan tried and failed to use the things of this world to have Jesus fall down and worship him.

Again, the devil taketh Him up into an exceed-ing high mountain, and sheweth Him all the king-doms of the world, and the glory of them; And saith unto Him, All these things will I give thee, if thou wilt fall down and worship me. (Matthew 4:8–9)

Notice that Satan was able to take Jesus to a place where He could view the entire world and all of the possessions gathered up in the nations before Him. Satan's strategy was to play on the human side of the Son of God and get Him to desire the things of this world more than His commitment to His Father in heaven. The devil has not changed. If he can get God's people so wrapped up in seeking the things of this world that they have no time for their service to their God, then he has achieved his goal. This was Satan's third attempt to sidetrack the Son of God. He saved what he thought was his most powerful temptation until last.

The allure of wealth and the love of money have destroyed the worship of many. The desire to get and maintain power and wealth has become their downfall, driving them to sacrifice their honor and integrity on the altar of greed. The driving force that pulls nations together is making alliances that will benefit them materially. Nations that abhor the attacks on human rights will ignore those attacks for economic gain.

China is a prime example of forced labor camps and sweat-shops, often using child labor to achieve greater levels of wealth for the Chinese Communist Party. America's trade with other nations is worth $4.9 trillion per year. China, Canada, and Mexico are the country's largest trading partners, accounting for $1.9 trillion worth of imports and exports (source: United States Census Bureau, Bureau of Economic Analysis 2016). We, as a nation, are eager to do business with a brutal communist dictatorship committing grave injustices to their own people because it benefits us materially. Jesus answered Satan concerning his last attempt to entice Him away from the ser-vice of His Heavenly Father.

Then saith Jesus unto him, Get thee hence, Satan: for it is written, Thou shalt worship the Lord thy God, and Him only shalt thou serve. (Matthew 4:10)

We must pause and ask ourselves as the children of God, "Am I controlling the desire for things in my walk with the Lord, or is the desire for things controlling me?"

Materialism

It is important to address this topic early on, realizing that it is a powerful driving force in our world today. I think it is safe to say that materialism has replaced God in many people's lives. We work to get things and then place importance of keeping those things before our service to God, turning these material possessions into idols. I remember my years of working in the automobile industry and the many times I was asked to work on Sunday and earn double pay. I rejected it because, as a Christian, I committed to keeping Sunday the Lord's Day by attending and serving in our local church.

Many individuals would work all the hours made available to them to earn more money. Having things is not a sin if those things do not become more important to us than our walk with the Lord. Satan delights in us when we place things before God. It is in our human nature to want what we don't have. In today's ever-changing world, we struggle to keep up with new technologies and all that is available to us in the marketplace. In the pursuit of material possessions, our nation has become more secular, deeming physical pleasures more important than spiritual values.

God makes it clear in His Word that it is He and He alone Who gives individuals the power to get wealth.

> *But thou shalt remember the LORD thy God:*
> *for it is He that giveth thee power to get wealth, that*
> *He may establish His covenant which He sware unto*
> *thy fathers, as it is this day. (Deuteronomy 8:18)*

God spoke through Moses to the nation of Israel prior to their entrance into the promised land. God warned them not to forget the one Who led them out of the bondage of Egypt, bringing them into the land of blessing.

> *Beware that thou forget not the LORD thy God, in not keeping His commandments, and His judgments, and His statutes, which I command thee this day: Lest when thou hast eaten and art full, and hast built goodly houses, and dwelt therein; And when thy herds and thy flocks multiply, and thy silver and thy gold is multiplied, and all that thou hast is multiplied; Then thine heart be lifted up, and thou forget the LORD thy God, which brought thee forth out of the land of Egypt, from the house of bondage; (Deuteronomy 8:11–14)*

The danger for us today is the same as it was for Israel in the past. When we have material abundance, our hearts can easily become lifted, forgetting the one who has blessed us and given us the power to get wealth. A famous king in the Old Testament learned this lesson the hard way. He became puffed up with himself and credited his wealth to his own power.

> *All this came upon the king Nebuchadnezzar. At the end of twelve months he walked in the palace of the kingdom of Babylon. The king spake, and said, Is not this great Babylon, that I have built for the house of the kingdom by the might of my power, and for the honour of my majesty? (Daniel 4:28–30)*

God spoke from heaven, informing the king that the kingdom would be taken from him, and in that same hour, he lost his mind and was driven out into the fields to dwell with the beasts, where he remained as a wild man under the dews of heaven for seven years.

America has been blessed by the hand of God and has lived in peace for most of its existence. Our young people have not experienced the horror of a world war as some of our past generations have. Our living standards have improved to the extent that most Americans can live in abundance, depending on their desire to work hard and get ahead. Opportunities abound in our nation for those who strive to improve themselves.

Most of our garages hold more than one vehicle (if they can be squeezed in around all the stuff), and most homes have multiple television sets and numerous electronic devices to keep our minds occupied. We have furnaces to keep us warm in the winter, air conditioners to keep us cool in the summer, and microwaves to make preparing our food a snap. The job market is booming, with employers competing for workers to fill their open positions. All of this should result in our nation being at peace and its citizens being happy and fulfilled in their daily lives.

However, we are constantly bombarded by news of mass shootings and drug overdoses. A number of our major cities are filled with crime and violence, with those in positions of authority incapable of bringing peace and order to the streets. Our national leaders blame our current condition on a myriad of different situations or on certain groups of individuals in our society. The truth of the matter is that, as a nation, we have turned away from God, and He is turning away from us. His warning to Israel rings loud and clear for America today. We must, as a nation, go back to our biblical foundation and to our God Who established us and has blessed us through these past years.

I have expounded on the subject of materialism because a nation living in abundance and relative peace with their physical needs being met can easily forget their God. The decisions being made by our national and local leaders are typically those involving economic improvement for those whom they serve. They know that these areas of emphasis are the ones that keep bringing voters their way. These decisions are focused on physical needs while ignoring our spiritual failures.

As an example, a study by the Guttmacher Institute found that the main reason given by women seeking an abortion (74 percent of 1209 patients interviewed) was that having a baby would interfere with the individual's education, work, or ability to care for dependents. These are obviously economic reasons to terminate the pregnancy without considering what God has said in His Word concerning human life. Let me be quick to add that God loves us and will forgive us for all our sins when we call upon Him through His Son, Jesus Christ. Abortion is a subject and study in itself. It is this author's position based on the Word of God that abortion is the murder of innocent life. I cover this subject more extensively in my book titled *Godly Priorities for Christian Living* available through the *Sword of the Lord.* I mention it here as an example of making decisions based on material versus spiritual values.

We could list many other ills in our society today that are weakening our nation, but most of them all come back to being self-focused and having the desire to fill our lives with this world's goods. We join gyms to build up our bodies, and we attend institutions of higher learning to strengthen our minds. These are good things to do, but if we neglect our soul and, in so doing, our spiritual walk with the Lord, we remain empty and continue to seek from this world that inner peace that it cannot provide. It would be better for us to live this life and walk in obedience to our Lord than to be rich in this world's goods and leave this life spiritually bankrupt. Having material possessions is a blessing if they don't become more important to us than our God.

Israel became wealthy in their new land and forgot God, bringing God's judgment down upon them. God's disappointment with His people is obvious in the following scriptures. They had been blessed by Him, but then they let themselves be pulled away by the world around them. God shares their story with us today as a warning not to follow their path, which brought the destruction of their once-great nation.

They have corrupted themselves, their spot is
not the spot of His children: they are a perverse and

> *crooked generation. Do ye thus requite the* LORD, *O foolish people and unwise? is not He thy father that hath bought thee? hath He not made thee, and established thee? (Deuteronomy 32:5–6)*

The word *requite* in the verse above means to pay back. Do we turn a blind eye to all that God has done for us and become self-absorbed, seeking all of life's pleasures while ignoring our worship and service to Him? The establishment of our nation has many similarities to the establishment of the nation of Israel. God led them out of Egypt to a new land, a land of promise, where they could worship Him and be blessed by Him. When the pilgrims came to our shores, they came seeking religious freedom to serve God apart from the dictates of the Church of England.

In that first brutal winter of 1620–1621, forty-five of the 102 *Mayflower* passengers died from lack of shelter, scurvy, and general conditions aboard the ship. Only fifty-three passengers and half the crew survived. Women were the hardest hit, with only five of the nineteen who boarded the ship surviving that first winter. When the group left the ship and went ashore, two to three people died each day. It was by God's grace that He sent an Indian named Squanto from the Powhatan tribe, who taught them how to survive the harsh New England weather.

Our nation's founding was wrought with hardship and sacrifice. But for the grace of our God and His care for those early pilgrims, America as we know it would not exist today. The following text describes God's establishment of the nation of Israel. He took them from a place of humble beginnings and made a mighty nation of them, keeping His promises to His servant Abraham.

> *He found him in a desert land, and in the waste howling wilderness; He led him about, He instructed him, He kept him as the apple of His eye. As an eagle stirreth up her nest, fluttereth over her young, spreadeth abroad her wings, taketh them, beareth them on her wings: So the* LORD *alone did*

lead him, and there was no strange god with him. He made him ride on the high places of the earth, that he might eat the increase of the fields; and He made him to suck honey out of the rock, and oil out of the flinty rock; Butter of kine, and milk of sheep, with fat of lambs, and rams of the breed of Bashan, and goats, with the fat of kidneys of wheat; and thou didst drink the pure blood of the grape. (Deuteronomy 32:10–14)

Israel became a nation greatly blessed by the hand of God. They were in their own land, living in peace, having all their needs met, and more. It would seem they would praise and serve their God for all His blessings bestowed upon them. But sad to say, when we as human beings have all that our hearts can desire, we begin focusing more on the things in our lives than on God, Who provided them for us.

But Jeshurun waxed fat, and kicked: thou art waxen fat, thou art grown thick, thou art covered with fatness; then he forsook God which made him, and lightly esteemed the Rock of his salvation. They provoked Him to jealousy with strange gods, with abominations provoked they Him to anger. They sacrificed unto devils, not to God; to gods whom they knew not, to new gods that came newly up, whom your fathers feared not. Of the Rock that begat thee thou art unmindful, and hast forgotten God that formed thee. (Deuteronomy 32:15–18)

Jeshurun is another name for Israel and means "the upright one." When Israel became prosperous, they forgot their God, forsook Him, and turned to the false idols of the nations around them. It is my firm belief that America, as a blessed nation by the hand of God, has become arrogant, turned its back on the God Who established it, and made it the envy of the world. As a nation, we have aligned ourselves with the ungodly kingdoms of this world for material gain. Israel provoked God to anger, and history tells the story of their defeat and dispersion at the hands of their enemies. God sent troubles from without and within, resulting in the demise of a once-great nation. America today is struggling with unrest within and fierce enemies without that seek our destruction. The hour is late, but there is still hope for our deliverance. The remainder of this book clearly lays out the necessary steps for our continued existence as a nation and on whose shoulders our future rests.

Who Is Responsible for Our Nation's Condition?

It is human nature to seek out and assign blame to those we believe to be responsible for the current state of affairs. It seems the first place to look is toward those holding office in our government. Whether it is at the national or local levels, it must be those in power who are causing all the chaos in our land.

As an example, in the state where I live, during the last governor's election, the candidate running against the incumbent blamed all the state's potholes and poor road conditions on the person currently holding office. They promised that if elected, they would fix all the roads and protect our vehicles in the process. At the national level, we blame the current administration for high rates of inflation, the cost of a gallon of gas, and the skyrocketing cost of groceries. We turn on the news each day and are overwhelmed with commentators laying blame on one political party or another. So who is actually at fault for our nation's current struggles?

It is true that those in office do, in fact, affect our lives through the policies they implement and the direction they take us. Their party affiliation has a lot to do with the decisions they make. There are vast differences in the thinking and practices between liberal and conservative politicians. During the campaign season, those seeking our support promise to do many wonderful things for us if we cast our vote their way. After the frenzy of the election has subsided, many times they forget those promises and govern differently.

On other occasions, we may blame the business people running some of our major organizations. As an example, we have heard our government leaders blame the petroleum producers for the high fuel prices. They are accused of being greedy and using the COVID-19 pandemic and its effects to gouge the public, increasing their profits during a time of national struggle. For the working class in our nation, Wall Street is responsible for holding the middle class down, preventing them from getting ahead and enjoying a higher standard of living.

So who is it that is most responsible for the current condition of our nation? We are struggling within against domestic violence and without against rogue nations seeking to destroy us. What I am about to say will, no doubt, shock some of you and may cause some to become upset against this author for proclaiming such a thing. The truth is that while these individuals and groups can at times trouble our country, they are not the ones who are actually responsible for our difficulties. The true culprits in all of this are we who identify ourselves as Christians. The blood-bought, Holy Spirit–filled children of God. That's right, God's people. We are never comfortable looking at ourselves and acknowledging the fact that it is the way we are living that is bringing hurt to our land. It broke the heart of God to turn away and permit the destruction of the children of Israel because of their backsliding and sinful ways. We hear the sorrow in His voice as He gives them over to the judgment to come.

> *And He said, I will hide my face from them, I will see what their end shall be: for they are a very froward generation, children in whom is no faith. For they are a nation void of counsel, neither is there any understanding in them. O that they were wise, that they understood this, that they would consider their latter end! (Deuteronomy 32:20, 28–29)*

The word *froward* in the above verse means "not willing to yield or comply with what is required or is reasonable." Other words used to describe this condition are *perverse, ungovernable, disobedient,* and *petulant.* God made it clear to Moses that after He blessed His people in the promised land, they would turn away from Him and seek after the ways of the world around them. The blessings of God upon a nation are entirely dependent on His children's worship and obedience toward Him.

> *Blessed is the nation whose God is the LORD;*
> *and the people whom He hath chosen for His own*
> *inheritance. (Psalm 33:12)*

I include the following lengthy portion of scripture to fully communicate God's promises to those who seek Him and to those who walk in obedience to His Word.

> *And it shall come to pass, if thou shalt harken diligently unto the voice of the LORD thy God, to observe and to do all His commandments which I command thee this day, that the LORD thy God will set thee on high above all nations of the earth: And all these blessings shall come on thee, and overtake thee, if thou shalt hearken unto the voice of the LORD thy God. Blessed shalt thou be in the city, and blessed shalt thou be in the field. Blessed shall be the fruit of thy body, and the fruit of thy ground, and the fruit of thy cattle, the increase of thy kine, and the flocks of thy sheep. Blessed shall be thy basket and thy store. Blessed shalt thou be when thou comest in, and blessed shalt thou be when thou goest out. The LORD shall cause thine enemies that rise up against thee to be smitten before thy face: they shall come out against thee one way, and flee before thee seven ways. The LORD shall command the blessing upon thee in thy storehouses, and in all that thou settest thine hand unto; and He shall bless thee in the land which the LORD thy God giveth thee. The LORD shall establish thee an holy people unto him-*

*self, as He hath sworn unto thee, if thou shalt keep
the commandments of the LORD thy God, and walk
in His ways. (Deuteronomy 28:1–9)*

These promises of God are still valid for us today. Notice the requirement for obtaining these blessings from the hand of God. There are three *if*s in the verses above. They direct us to harken (listen) to the voice of our God and then to keep His commandments. When we, as the children of God, hear His voice and obey it, He will pour out His blessings upon our land.

*The LORD shall establish thee an holy people
unto himself, as He hath sworn unto thee, if thou
shalt keep the commandments of the LORD thy God,
and walk in His ways. (Deuteronomy 28:9)*

Amen and amen! Notice that this precious promise from our Lord is predicated upon our keeping His commandments and walking in His ways, not our own. I believe one of the greatest portions of scripture that communicate to us our responsibilities as the children of God is found in the verses below.

*If my people, which are called by my name,
shall humble themselves, and pray, and seek my face,
and turn from their wicked ways; then will I hear
from heaven, and will forgive their sin, and will
heal their land. Now mine eyes shall be open, and
mine ears attent unto the prayer that is made in this
place. (2 Chronicles 7:14–15)*

It is we, the people of God, who are primarily responsible for the condition of our nation. His promises are still valid for us today. His blessings are still available to us if we will hear His voice and obey His Word. President Truman once stated, "The buck stops here." He claimed full responsibility for the decisions he made as our leader. He placed a sign on his desk with this statement, reflecting his belief that he was ultimately responsible for the actions of his administration. God is calling upon His people in the text above to do four things to allow Him to heal their land. Humble themselves before Him (admit they have a need), pray (make their needs known to Him), seek His face (return to Him), and turn (repent) from their sins. As I stated earlier in this chapter, it is the lives of God's people that allow Him to bless or send judgment upon their land. We must enter a time of self-examination. David cried out in *Psalm 139:23–24,*

> *Search me, O God, and know my heart: try me, and know my thoughts: And see if there be any wicked way in me, and lead me in the way everlasting.*

David made the following commitment to God in *Psalm 51:10–13,*

> *Create in me a clean heart, O God; and renew a right spirit within me. Cast me not away from thy presence; and take not thy Holy Spirit from me. Restore unto me the joy of thy salvation; and uphold me with thy free spirit. Then will I teach transgressors thy ways; and sinners shall be converted unto thee.*

Christian, what is in your life today? What lies deeply within your heart? What would God find there if this were your prayer to Him in this moment? We are responsible for the health of our families and our homeland. Can we say along with President Truman that "the buck stops here"?

We are witnessing a severe decline in those attending church in our nation. In a 2020 survey conducted by the Pew Research Center, 65 percent of adults in America identified themselves as Christians, with only 37 percent of those attending church on a weekly basis. A new study from Lifeway Research revealed that more Protestant churches closed in 2019 than opened. They reported 4,500 closures versus 3,000 that opened. The study estimated that in the decade ending in 2020, there were 3,850–7,700 houses of worship closed per year in the United States, or 75–150 congregations per week. Gallup found that fewer than half (47 percent) of Americans say they belong to a church, synagogue, or mosque. This is down from more than 70 percent in 2000, which equates to a 23 percent decline in the last twenty years.

We need to earnestly pray for a heaven-sent, Holy Spirit–filled revival to sweep across our land. We need the touch of God's hand upon our nation once again. This requires all of God's children to get down on their knees and get right with Him. Whether it's the pursuit of this world's goods or other things that have entered our lives and turned our hearts away from our God, we must humble ourselves and return to Him if America is to be saved.

In Ezekiel chapter 8, the prophet was caught up by the hair of his head and was transported by an angelic being to Jerusalem in a vision. There, he was shown the wickedness of God's people as they worshipped the sun and all sorts of false idols, even painting pictures of these things on the walls inside the temple of God. As a result, God sent angelic beings throughout the city of Jerusalem, slaying all those who worshipped their false idols. In the New Testament, Peter referred to this event in *1 Peter 4:17.*

> *For the time is come that judgment must begin at the house of God: and if it first begin at us, what shall the end be of them that obey not the Gospel of God?*

We, as God's children, must look at our own lives first and get right with Him if we have drifted away into sin and wrongdoing. America needs us to stand firm upon the solid foundation of God's Holy Word and walk in obedience to Him, seeking His forgiveness of our sins and His hand of blessing upon our nation. Ezekiel watched in the vision as the angelic beings of God began purging the wickedness from the house of God and then proceeding throughout the city of Jerusalem.

What Is America's Greatest Need?

As 2 Chronicles 7:14 has stated, it is the lifestyle and the worship of God's children that make a difference in their nation. The Old Testament is very clear that when God's people were living in obedience to His Word and seeking Him with all their hearts, they were blessed. When they turned away from Him, the nation suffered, and many times, God permitted their enemies to come in and destroy them.

America's greatest need is for the blood-bought, born-again children of God to repent from their sins, humble themselves before Him, and plead for His grace and mercy to be poured out upon their land. We need to pray for those in leadership positions, whether or not we agree with their policies. We must pray that God will touch their hearts with the gospel of salvation and turn them toward Himself. We are in a battle between light and darkness. The forces of evil seek our destruction, and we must fight this battle on our knees. I firmly believe that God is in control and will do exactly what His Word says. He will not fail us in our time of need if we call upon Him from a pure heart and have a right spirit within us.

Getting right with God is serious business. It requires turning from our sins and walking in complete obedience to His Word. The book of Ezra gives us a powerful insight into what real repentance and turning back to God require. The people of Judah had been carried away into Babylon and were there for seventy years in exile. God touched the heart of a Persian gentile king named Cyrus to let the Jews who were so inclined go back to Jerusalem and rebuild the temple of God that had been destroyed during the last Babylonian incursion. Sadly enough, only a small remnant agreed to go back and engage in the rebuilding project. The exiles had gotten over the initial shock of being carried from their land into Babylon and had become comfortable there. They had begun to prosper and provide for themselves nice homes, and they resisted giving those things up to return to the broken-down city of Jerusalem. They had become comfortable and prosperous, living in the gentile world. A small remnant under the leadership of Zerubbabel returned to Jerusalem in about 536 BC and laid the foundation for the temple project. Approximately seventy-eight years later, Ezra the priest returned with another small group and restored temple worship and ritual. Soon thereafter, there arose a significant issue, requiring Ezra and the men of Judah to make a very difficult decision if, indeed, the nation was to get right with God.

> *Now when these things were done, the princes came to me, saying, The people of Israel, and the priests, and the Levites, have not separated themselves from the people of the lands, doing according to their abominations, even of the Canaanites, the Hittites, the Perizzites, the Jebusites, the Ammonites, the Moabites, the Egyptians and the Amorites. For they have taken of their daughters for themselves, and for their sons: so that the holy seed have mingled themselves with the people of those lands: yea, the hand of the princes and rulers hath been chief in this trespass. (Ezra 9:1–2)*

The sin in the above situation was that of God's chosen people becoming mixed up with the nations around them and getting caught up in their idolatrous ways. They were intermarrying and, in so doing, were becoming more like the world around them and less attentive to the separated life that God had called them to. Notice that both the political and religious leaders were caught up in this lifestyle. We see a close correlation to our world today. This could have been a result of them becoming comfortable in Babylon and then bringing some of those traits back to Jerusalem with them.

We must take all sin and backsliding seriously if we are, indeed, to return to the place of worship and fellowship with our Lord. It is not God Who has moved away from us. We have moved away from Him as a nation. In 1962, the US Supreme Court ruled that the Establishment Clause prohibited the recitation of a school-sponsored prayer in public schools. As a result of this ruling, our children were no longer able to pray as a group in the classroom as part of an opening ceremony prior to class work beginning.

In 1980, the US Supreme Court struck down a Kentucky statute that mandated every public school classroom have the Ten Commandments posted on its walls. The ruling came to prevent public schools from displaying the Ten Commandments year-round. As a result, God's Word was not allowed to be visible in the public school. Since that time, Christian students have continued to be ostracized for praying or taking their Bibles to school, even if they are engaging in these activities during their free time.

Without plunging into a deep history lesson (which is very tempting), we know that there is no such clause in the Constitution stating that there should be a wall of separation between the church and state. That phrase was erroneously lifted and completely misunderstood from a letter that Thomas Jefferson wrote to the Danbury Baptist on January 1, 1802. President Jefferson was responding to their letter to him with concerns that the government would involve itself in the free exercise of religion. He responded to them, assuring them with these words:

> I contemplate with the sovereign reverence
> that act of the whole American people which
> declared that their legislature should make no law
> respecting an establishment of religion or prohib-
> iting the free exercise thereof, thus building a wall
> of separation between Church and State.

Thomas Jefferson had no intention of allowing the government to limit, restrict, regulate, or interfere with public religious practices. As a result of the Court completely misapplying his comments, prayer and God's Word were removed from our schools, and our freedom of religious expression continues to be repressed today in the public square. Since removing God's influence from our young people's lives, we have experienced a greater degree of violence in our society, along with school shootings and the loss of respect for others. The deterioration of the educational materials being taught to our young people has ushered in a plague of moral decline and humanistic philosophy to the hurt and detriment of future generations.

Returning to our dilemma in Jerusalem, what was Ezra's reaction to this situation of God's people becoming mixed up with the world around them?

> *And when I heard this thing, I rent my garment and my mantle, and plucked off the hair of my head and of my beard, and sat down astonied. Then were assembled unto me every one that trembled at the words of the God of Israel, because of the transgression of those that had been carried away; and I sat astonied until the evening sacrifice. (Ezra 9:3–4)*

The word *astonied* is the Hebrew word *shamem*. It means to be appalled or stunned. Until our sins bring upon us an utter state of remorse and astonishment, we will continue in our present condition. Ezra displayed complete remorse for the spiritual condition of God's people. The Word of God brought great convicting power upon those sitting with Ezra. They were fully aware of their transgressions against the God of heaven.

America's greatest need is for God's people to enter into a time of self-examination, comparing our lives to the Word of God and openly confessing any sins that we are involved in. There are sins of commission, and then there are others referred to as sins of omission. We either do those things that God's Word teaches us not to do or we neglect to do other things that God has instructed us to do. Either way, we need to have a time of reflection and examine ourselves in light of God's direction for our lives.

Serious times require serious actions. The remnant of the exiled people had returned to Jerusalem, but they were not right with God and risked further judgment coming their way. Ezra's position as priest over them was put to the test. The people, recognizing the danger they were in because of their sins, came to him, urging him to intercede on their behalf and take the necessary actions to remove their sins.

> *Now when Ezra had prayed, and when he had confessed, weeping and casting himself down before the house of God, there assembled unto him out of Israel a very great congregation of men and women and children: for the people wept very sore. And Shechaniah the son of Jehiel, one of the sons of Elam, answered and said unto Ezra, We have trespassed against our God, and have taken strange wives of the people of the land: yet now there is hope in Israel concerning this thing. (Ezra 10:1–2)*

Notice that there was deep sorrow in the hearts of the people because of their sins. Before we can receive a true heaven-sent revival in our own lives or in our nation as a whole, we must come to God with open hearts, confess our sins, and seek His forgiveness. We find a wonderful promise from God's Word in the following verses:

> *This then is the message which we have heard of Him, and declare unto you, that God is light, and in Him is no darkness at all. If we say that we have fellowship with Him, and walk in darkness, we lie, and do not the truth: But if we walk in the light, as He is in the light, we have fellowship one with another, and the blood of Jesus Christ His Son cleanseth us from all sin. If we say that we have no sin, we deceive ourselves, and the truth is not in us. If we confess our sins, He is faithful and just to forgive us our sins, and to cleanse us from all*

unrighteousness. If we say that we have not sinned, we make Him a liar, and His Word is not in us. (1 John 1:5–10)

When we humble ourselves, pray, seek God's face, and turn from our wicked ways, God has promised to hear us from heaven, forgive us our sins, and heal our land. Dear brothers and sisters in Christ, America needs us now more than ever to be right with God, walking in obedience with Him in the light of His Holy Word. The message of the people to Ezra was that there was still hope in Israel concerning this thing. I fully believe there is hope for America in our current situation. It requires all of us, as God's children, to seek Him with all our hearts and live for Him every day.

The end of the situation with Ezra and the people of God at Jerusalem was the putting away of the strange wives and children they had taken to themselves. This seems harsh from a human perspective, but from a spiritual consideration, all sin must be dealt with in its entirety if we are going to be blessed by God. God's children have always been called to a place of separation in their service to Him.

Wherefore come out from among them, and be ye separate, saith the Lord, and touch not the unclean thing; and I will receive you, And will be a Father unto you, and ye shall be my sons and daughters, saith the Lord Almighty. (2 Corinthians 6:17–18)

As the children of God, we must not waver in these days of adversity but remain firmly anchored upon the solid rock of His Holy Word. Stand your ground where God has placed you, and be strong in the power of His might.

Biblical Examples for Our Admonition

Perhaps one of the saddest stories in the Bible is found in Exodus chapter 32. Moses had been up on Mount Sinai for forty days, and the impatience and spiritual immaturity of God's people were on full display. They murmured and complained once again against the leadership of Moses and Aaron, whom God had placed over them. They demanded that Aaron make them gods to lead them in Moses's absence. Aaron gave in to their demands and cast a golden calf, and then they sat down to eat, drink, and worship before it.

These are the same people who had passed through the Red Sea and walked on the dry ground, looking at the massive walls of water held up around them by the power of God's hand. They watched at Marah as Moses cast a tree into the bitter waters, turning them sweet for their consumption. They were witnesses of God's provision again as Moses struck the rock in Horeb and water poured forth, supplying all the needs of the people and their animals. They were given manna from heaven to eat, and their shoes did not wear out on their feet. They watched as Joshua fought the battle with Amalek in the valley with Moses on the hill, seated upon a rock with his hands held high to heaven, resulting in God giving a great victory in the battle that day. They saw the mighty power and presence of God on top of Mount Sinai, which appeared to them as a devouring fire.

After all that God had done in their lives, they turned from Him, with Moses up on the mount, and demanded a false god of gold be hammered out for them to worship instead of the God of heaven. We might pause and ask ourselves, How could these people have been so foolish? How could they have experienced all of God's blessings and then turned their backs on Him? Keep in mind that this turning away happened after only forty days of Moses going into the mount. Their change of heart took place in a very short time. But wait. We should not be so quick to judge them without looking at our own lives today as a nation that has been greatly blessed by God.

As we discussed in the second chapter of this book, America today is caught up in materialism and heavily involved in self-accommodation. Whether it's our sports addiction, use of mood-altering prescription drugs or hallucinating substances, or our desire for material possessions, we have in many ways turned our backs on our Lord for personal pleasure and gain.

Before we look at God's judgment brought against His people for their sins, let's consider the failure of those who were in leadership positions. Moses immediately took the necessary actions to purge the camp of the sin brought about by Aaron's weakness in life.

> *And it came to pass, as soon as he came nigh unto the camp, that he saw the calf, and the dancing: and Moses' anger waxed hot, and he cast the tables out of his hands, and brake them beneath the mount. And he took the calf which they had made, and burnt it in the fire, and ground it to powder, and strawed it upon the water, and made the children of Israel drink of it. And Moses said unto Aaron, What did this people unto thee, that thou hast brought so great a sin upon them? (Exodus 32:19–21)*

Notice that Moses did what was right in the sight of God by quickly becoming righteously indignant because of the sins of the people. Afterward, he turned his attention to his brother, Aaron, who would later become the high priest of Israel and be responsible for leading the nation in its spiritual walk with God. Aaron's feeble response is like many in our world today when they are caught up in wrongdoing. It's not my fault. It's the fault of the people around me. They made me do it.

> *And Aaron said, Let not the anger of my lord wax hot: thou knowest the people, that they are set on mischief. For they said unto me, Make us gods, which shall go before us: for as for this Moses, the man that brought us up out of the land of Egypt, we wot not what is become of him. And I said unto them, Whosoever hath any gold, let them break it off. So they gave it me: then I cast it into the fire, and there came out this calf. (Exodus 32:22–24)*

Aaron readily acknowledged the leadership of Moses as his lord, but he passed all responsibility for the creation of the false god onto the people themselves. He also lied about how the calf came into existence by claiming it came out of the fire on its own accord. Notice that the people credited Moses for bringing them out of Egypt and not the God of heaven. When grave mistakes have been made, those responsible must be willing to confess their wrongdoing and repent of their failures. Sins of wrongdoing cannot be cleansed without heartfelt confession and repentance, seeking God's forgiveness. After a moral and spiritual failure of this magnitude, serious decisions must be made.

What direction would they go from that day forward? Today, as a nation, we have sinned against our God by taking innocent lives and calling it a choice. Among many other wrongdoings, we have condoned the evil of sexual perversion to go along and get along. Are we willing, as a people, to come back to God, submit ourselves to His leadership, and walk in obedience to His Word? The end of that sad day in Israel's history is told in the actions that Moses took to purge the nation of its sin.

> *Then Moses stood in the gate of the camp, and said, Who is on the LORD's side? let him come unto me. And all the sons of Levi gathered them-*

selves together unto him. And he said unto them, Thus saith the LORD God of Israel, Put every man his sword by his side, and go in and out from gate to gate throughout the camp, and slay every man his brother, and every man his companion, and every man his neighbor. And the children of Levi did according to the word of Moses: and there fell of the people that day about three thousand men. (Exodus 32:26–28)

Moses saw that the wickedness of the people that day was great. He thus ordered the sons of Levi to enter the camp and slay those who were apparently the ringleaders encouraging the sinful acts. The people had made themselves naked (if not completely, at least partially so), played loud music, and danced indecently before their false god. Sinful acts always bring destruction to those caught up in them. The screaming of those being killed and the terror of those looking on were burned into their minds for the rest of their lives. What a horrifying scene that must have been.

Our God is a holy God and will not tolerate sin among His people. For a nation to be blessed by Him, they must be willing to repent, put away their sinful ways, and walk in obedience to Him. I pray that our nation will return to our God with tears of repentance before it is too late. We, as His children, are responsible for seeking His face and walking in the light before Him. We can ask ourselves the same question that Moses asked the people of Israel that fateful day: "Who is on the Lord's side?"

Dear brothers and sisters in Christ, my prayer for you is that you will be the ones to crossover and make a firm commitment to the Lord today, committing yourselves to stay firmly on His side. His grace and His mercy are richly available to us today if we will reach out to Him. He loves us unconditionally and wants to have uninterrupted fellowship with us, showering heaven's blessings down upon us.

Before we leave this area of study, there are some additional lessons to be learned that can be applied to our lives today. Where were these men of Levi when Aaron was being pressured to give the people their wicked desire that day? Why didn't they come alongside Aaron and rebuke the people for their evil request to make their voices known? Could it have been that they were fearful of the hordes calling out loudly in pursuit of their rebellion against the authority that God had placed over them and against God Himself? If they had stood with Aaron against those demands, could their actions that day have spared the three thousand who died as a consequence of their wickedness? The lesson for all of God's children is that we must speak out to our leaders who are being pressured to implement wrong-doing in our society and strongly encourage them to choose right over wrong. We must lift our voices in opposition to the throngs clambering for sin and debauchery in our day. We need to pray for our leaders and let them know that we support them when they lead according to the law and righteousness.

The men of Levi failed their duty on that fateful day. Their silence resulted in the death and destruction that perhaps could have been avoided. The church of Jesus Christ must make its presence known in our world today. We must stand firmly upon the Holy Word of our God and not remain silent.

Another biblical example given to us in God's Word is found in Nehemiah chapter 3. I must admit that when I come to one of these chapters where God reveals to me long lists of genealogies, it becomes difficult to concentrate on all the *begats* throughout the verses. Having said this, we know that God has put every word in our Bible for His own eternal purpose and for our edification. In the case of Nehemiah chapter 3, God provides us with an exact record of the children of Israel who returned to Jerusalem and engaged in the rebuilding of the walls under Nehemiah's leadership. One event that God records here could be easily overlooked. There were certain individuals who did not participate in the work.

And next unto them the Tekoites repaired; but their nobles put not their necks to the work of their Lord. (Nehemiah 3:5)

We are not sure who these nobles were. One thing we are sure of is the fact that they did not get involved in the work going on around them. They would, however, benefit later from the labor of those who did join in the effort. On the other hand, God documents the name of a man who was in a leadership position himself who rolled up his sleeves and labored with the builders, along with his daughters by his side.

> *And next unto him repaired Shallum the son*
> *of Halohesh, the ruler of the half part of Jerusalem,*
> *he and his daughters. (Nehemiah 3:12)*

God documented for an eternal testimony the workers who joined in the effort to rebuild the walls of the city, and He also noted the ones who sat idly by letting others complete the task at hand. God placed these verses in His Word, revealing to us that He knows exactly who is laboring for Him and who is not. The day is coming when all of us must give an account of ourselves before Him.

> *For it is written, As I live, saith the Lord, every*
> *knee shall bow to me, and every tongue shall confess*
> *to God. So then every one of us shall give account of*
> *himself to God. (Romans 14:11–12)*

It is critical that we labor for our Lord while we have the opportunity, realizing there is a day of accounting coming for all of us. God also keeps perfect records of His children's service to Him so they may be rewarded for their labor.

> *For other foundation can no man lay than that*
> *is laid, which is Jesus Christ. Now if any man build*
> *upon this foundation gold, silver, precious stones,*
> *wood, hay, stubble; Every man's work shall be made*
> *manifest: for the day shall declare it, because it shall*
> *be revealed by fire; and the fire shall try every man's*
> *work of what sort it is. If any man's work abide*

which he hath built thereupon, he shall receive a reward. If any man's work shall be burned, he shall suffer loss: but he himself shall be saved; yet so as by fire. (1 Corinthians 3:11–15)

God is a God of records. His heart desires to reward His children for their labor for Him. It is a joy to serve Him, knowing that He notices when we give as much as a glass of water in His name (Mark 9:41). Let me be quick to say that we serve Him because we love Him, not because we are seeking rewards for ourselves. But the knowledge that our labors are not in vain brings us joy in our service to Him.

God also keeps perfect records of all our sins if they have not been forgiven through the blood of Jesus that was shed on the cross for us. I would be remiss if I didn't emphasize here the importance of repenting of your sins and receiving Jesus Christ as your personal Lord and Saviour. As there is a day of accounting for God's children for their service to Him, there is also a day of accounting for all those who have not received forgiveness of their sins through Christ's atoning death for them.

And I saw the dead small and great, stand before God; and the books were opened: and another book was opened, which is the book of life: and the dead were judged out of those things which were written in the books, according to their works. And the sea gave up the dead which were in it; and death and hell delivered up the dead which were in them: and they were judged every man according to their works. And death and hell were cast into the lake of fire. This is the second death. And whosoever was not found written in the book of life was cast into the lake of fire. (Revelation 20:12–15)

This book is written primarily as a discipleship tool for Christians, but if you are reading this and have not received Jesus as your Saviour or if you are not sure if you died today you would go to heaven, I urge you to make that decision while there is still time. God loves you, and He will forgive you of all your sins and wipe them from His record book forever through the blood of His precious Son. The book of life in the verse above is the book in which God's children are recorded. The moment you trust Jesus as your Lord and Saviour, God enters your name in His book of eternal life. He receives all who call upon Him and who repent of their sins, and He will in no way refuse anyone who comes to Him.

> *All that the Father giveth me shall come to me; and him that cometh to me I will in no wise cast out. (John 6:37)*

> *For whosoever shall call upon the name of the Lord shall be saved. (Romans 10:13)*

You can pray and be saved at this moment if you call upon the Saviour. I urge you to make this critical decision without delay. Your eternal soul depends on it.

Dear Lord Jesus, I am a sinner. Please forgive me of my sins and give me a home in heaven. I believe You are the Son of God. I am trusting in Your shed blood on the cross to save me and take away my sin. I open my heart and receive You as my personal Lord and Saviour. I will follow You as my Lord from this day forward. Thank You, Jesus, for saving my soul. I pray and ask this in Your name, AMEN.

> *These things have I written unto you that believe on the name of the Son of God; that ye may know that ye have eternal life, and that ye may believe on the name of the Son of God. (1 John 5:13)*

If you have made a decision for Christ, I encourage you to seek out a local New Testament gospel-preaching church where you can learn God's Word and walk in obedience to Him.

> *Not forsaking the assembling of ourselves together, as the manner of some is; but exhorting one another: and so much the more, as ye see the day approaching. (Hebrews 10:25)*

Going to God's house allows us to fellowship with other brothers and sisters in Christ and be encouraged in our walk with Him. Our attendance is especially important as the day of Jesus's return draws near.

How Much Time Do We Have Left?

It is an undisputable biblical fact that this world as we know it is coming to an end. Jesus is coming again to call His children home and to judge this world for its sin. Jesus was celebrating His last Passover with His disciples when He encouraged them not to be troubled because of the hatred toward Him coming from the religious leaders in Jerusalem. He spoke to them, giving them hope for the future that He would return one day and take them home to heaven to be with Him for all eternity. That same hope is ours today as we await our Master's call.

> *Let not your heart be troubled: ye believe in God, believe also in me. In my Father's house are many mansions: if it were not so, I would have told you. I go to prepare a place for you. And if I go and prepare a place for you, I will come again, and receive you unto myself; that where I am, there ye may be also. (John 14:1–3)*

Our Lord's second coming is in two parts. First, to call his children out of this world in the rapture of the church, and second, to return at the end of the battle of Armageddon that occurs at the end of the seven-year tribulation on earth. Following these events, Jesus will establish His one-thousand-year kingdom, ruling this earth from His throne in Jerusalem. None of us know when the rapture of the church will take place. There have been many date-setters in the past, and all of them have been proven wrong. Jesus Himself, when He was on earth, was asked when the end would come. He responded that only God, His Father, possessed that knowledge.

> *But of that day and hour knoweth no man,*
> *no, not the angels of heaven, but my Father only.*
> *(Matthew 24:36)*

God tells us in His Word to be ever watching and waiting, for we know neither the day nor the hour in which our Lord will come. Let's examine Jesus's second coming in two parts. It is important for the children of God to be prepared for their meeting with Him in the air. This is the first advent of His return and will only involve born-again Christians who make up His New Testament church here on earth.

> *Behold, I shew you a mystery; We shall not all*
> *sleep, but we shall all be changed, In a moment,*
> *in the twinkling of an eye, at the last trump: for*
> *the trumpet shall sound, and the dead shall be*
> *raised incorruptible, and we shall be changed. For*
> *this corruptible must put on incorruption, and this*
> *mortal must put on immortality. (1 Corinthians*
> *15:51–53)*

The apostle Paul wrote two letters to the church at Corinth, addressing doctrinal problems in the church. Among other issues, some spoke against the resurrection from the dead. In the above verse, the word *sleep* is the Greek word *koimao*, which is used here in reference to a dead person. Paul is clearly teaching that there is coming a time when the dead shall be raised back to life and those still alive shall be changed. He states that this will happen in a moment in the twinkling of an eye. That is an instantaneous event. In the blink of an eye, our transformation will occur—from these mortal, sin-ridden bodies to new spiritual bodies that have never known sin. He continued this teaching to the church at

Thessalonica, clearly assuring us of our future meeting with our Lord in the air.

> *But I would not have you to be ignorant, brethren, concerning them which are asleep, that ye sorrow not, even as others which have no hope. For if we believe that Jesus died and rose again, even so them also which sleep in Jesus will God bring with Him. For this we say unto you by the word of the Lord, that we which are alive and remain unto the coming of the Lord shall not prevent them which are asleep. For the Lord Himself shall descend from heaven with a shout, with the voice of the archangel, and with the trump of God: and the dead in Christ shall rise first: Then we which are alive and remain shall be caught up together with them in the clouds, to meet the Lord in the air: and so shall we ever be with the Lord. Wherefore comfort one another with these words. (1 Thessalonians 4:13–18)*

Notice that Paul believed this would occur in his lifetime. He included himself among the living when this great event would take place. Paul was constantly watching and waiting for his Lord's return to take him home. To answer the question concerning how much time we have left as Christians, we must conclude based on God's Word that we could be called up to meet our Lord in the air at any moment in the twinkling of an eye. For God's children awaiting the rapture, God encourages us to recognize the time in which we're living and be prepared to meet Him at His coming.

> *And that, knowing the time, that now it is high time to awake out of sleep: for now is our salvation nearer than when we believed. The night is far spent, the day is at hand: let us therefore cast off the works of darkness; and let us put on the armour of light. (Romans 13:11–12)*

If we are truly watching, waiting, and expecting His return at any moment, it should cause us to walk close to our Saviour every day, doing those things that are right and acceptable in His sight.

In the second part of our Lord's return, He physically touches down on the top of the Mount of Olives at the end of the seven-year tribulation and marches into battle against the wicked that remained on the earth after the rapture of the church.

God's Word gives us some insight into this world's condition that would indicate when this second part of His return would be near. Matthew 24 is known as the Olivet Discourse and is eschatological in nature (focused on future events). This chapter is written for the Jewish nation and focuses on the events coming against them during the tribulation. The disciples ask Jesus a very important question.

> *And as He sat upon the Mount of Olives, the disciples came unto Him privately, saying, Tell us, when shall these things be? and what shall be the sign of thy coming, and of the end of the world? (Matthew 24:3)*

Jesus had just concluded telling them of the future destruction of the temple when they asked Him this question. He gave them two important pieces of information concerning this world's condition just prior to His physical return to the earth at the end of the seven-year tribulation.

> *And as it was in the days of Noe, so shall it be also in the days of the Son of man. They did eat, they drank, they married wives, they were given in marriage, until the day that Noe entered into the ark, and the flood came, and destroyed them all. (Luke 17:26–27)*

People were going about their lives and ignoring the coming judgment of God. Noah was a preacher of righteousness and preached for one hundred twenty years without a convert apart from the members of his own family. The world went about its business, ignoring him and his Bible messages. They were busy with weddings, building homes, striving to get ahead, obtaining material possessions, and planning for their future. The Word of God tells us that the earth was also filled with violence during Noah's day.

> *And God saw that the wickedness of man was great in the earth, and that every imagination of the thoughts of his heart was only evil continually. And it repented the LORD that He had made man on the earth, and it grieved Him at His heart. And the Lord said, I will destroy man whom I have created from the face of the earth; both man, and beast, and the creeping thing, and the fowls of the air; for it repenteth me that I have made them. (Genesis 6:5–7)*

The second example that Jesus gave His disciples was that of Lot, Abraham's nephew.

> *Likewise also as it was in the days of Lot; they did eat, they drank, they bought, they sold, they planted, they builded; But the same day that Lot went out of Sodom it rained fire and brimstone from heaven, and destroyed them all. Even thus shall it be in the day when the Son of man is revealed. (Luke 17:28–29)*

Notice that Lot's day closely resembled that of Noah's time. People were going about their everyday lives, ignoring God as if there was no pending judgment for the wickedness filling their hearts.

> *But the men of Sodom were wicked and sinners before the Lord exceedingly. (Genesis 13:13)*

We know that the sin in Sodom and Gomorrah was homosexuality and sexual perversion. God sent two angels there to bring Lot and his family out of the city before God destroyed the place. The men of the city sought to have sex with them, demanding that Lot send them out from his home to them. The angels removed Lot and his wife and two daughters from the wicked place, and then God sent down His judgment upon it.

> *Then the LORD rained upon Sodom and upon Gomorrah brimstone and fire from the LORD out of heaven; And He overthrew those cities, and all the plain, and all the inhabitants of the cities, and that which grew upon the ground. (Genesis 19:24–25)*

How much time do we have left? We have learned the answer in the above scriptures concerning Jesus's second coming. First, in the air for His church, which can happen at any moment in the twinkling of an eye, and then second, at the end of the tribulation period when people are least expecting it and going about their daily lives. As I wrote this chapter, I quickly realized that the events prior to Jesus's physical return to the earth at the end of the tribulation are already present in our world today. Attendance at the house of God has continued to decrease while the materialistic desires of the people have increased. God's Word has been cast aside as people pursue their day-to-day lives as if time would never end and a future judgment day would never arrive.

We see violence continue to rise as death and destruction fill many of our nation's cities, with our children losing their lives as a result of going to school. Sexual perversion is running rampant in our society today and has even invaded our children's schools at the lowest grade levels, teaching them that they can be a girl, a boy, or have no sex at all and simply think of themselves as "it." Transgenderism, along with cross-dressing, has been encouraged in certain instances, and in others, drag queens have been invited to speak to our children at school and public libraries. The government and businesses alike have made laws and special provisions for individuals who display their sexual deviancy and threaten those who stand up and oppose it.

We know that the above will be the condition of this world just prior to Jesus's physical return to the earth. If these things are occurring today and reflect the state of affairs at the end of the seven-year tribulation, how close must we be to the rapture of the church calling God's children home? I pray that this observation will impress upon all our hearts the urgency of the time in which we live. The last chapter of this book reveals God's desire for His children at times such as these.

Salt and Light

> *Ye are the salt of the earth: but if the salt have lost his savour, wherewith shall it be salted? it is thenceforth good for nothing, but to be cast out, and to be trodden under foot of men. Ye are the light of the world. A city that is set on an hill cannot be hid. Neither do men light a candle, and put it under a bushel, but on a candlestick: and it giveth light unto all that are in the house. Let your light so shine before men, that they may see your good works, and glorify your Father which is in heaven. (Matthew 5:13–16)*

Jesus spoke these words as He sat, teaching His disciples on the mount. Jesus knew that one day, He would return to His Father in heaven, and they would be left on earth to carry the message of salvation to those lost in sin. Salt is a purifying agent, and light drives out darkness.

I can remember, as a young boy growing up on our West Tennessee cotton farm, that my father would kill the hogs in the fall, salt down the meat, and hang it in the smokehouse. The salt served as an agent to preserve the meat and prevent it from spoiling. The salt that my father used was fresh and carried within it the power to make a difference.

Jesus warned His disciples that if the salt lost its savor, it was good for nothing but to be cast out and trodden under the feet of men. The word *savor* is defined as something that has the quality, or ability, to perceptibly affect the sense of taste and smell. It must have the strength to make a difference and make others aware of its presence. For God's children to make a difference, we must be operating at full strength and spiritually walking in obedience to His Word in a sin-laden world.

> WHEREFORE seeing we also are compassed about with so great a cloud of witnesses, let us lay aside every weight, and the sin which doth so easily beset us, and let us run with patience the race that is set before us. (Hebrews 12:1)

The weight that Paul was referring to was that of worldly encumbrances. He warned us against permitting this world's distractions to fill our lives to such a degree that we have no time left to serve our Lord. The sin that he refers to is that of walking in disobedience to God's Word. Paul taught that both of these things must be avoided in the lives of God's children if we are to effectively win lost souls to Him. Falling prey to either of these takes away the power of our testimony and, along with it, the power to make a difference in the lives of others around us. Those with whom we come into contact must sense that there is something pure and powerful within us that can affect their lives positively. The strength and power of your testimony are the salt within you that can make a difference for our Lord.

Some years ago, I brought a message to our Sunday evening service and then went to the back of the chapel to shake hands with those leaving when an elderly man seated near the back motioned me to him. He said to me, "I want what you all have."

I asked what it was we had that he wanted.

With tears in his eyes, he said, "The joy and happiness in your lives, the way that you smile and worship the Lord, the feeling of peace that I find in this place."

I drew a chair up next to him and shared the gospel of Jesus, and I was blessed to lead him in the sinner's prayer. He received Jesus as his Saviour that night and was gloriously saved. Radiance came over his face when we finished praying, and we sat hugging each other as others gathered around and rejoiced over one who had been lost but had now found their way home. I was asked a few years later to preach at that man's funeral, where his family testified that after his salvation decision, he had become a new man, rejoicing in his walk with the Lord with his witness and making a difference in their lives along the way.

The apostle Paul, by the inspiration of the Holy Spirit, taught that we are ambassadors for Christ.

> *Now then we are ambassadors for Christ, as though God did beseech you by us: we pray you in Christ's stead, be ye reconciled to God. (2 Corinthians 5:20)*

An ambassador is appointed by the leader of their nation to go to a foreign country and represent their homeland to the people there. They are to show forth the values of their leader and their people to the nation to which they are sent. They do not represent themselves to the foreign country but rather the leader, who sent them. We can readily understand from this verse that we are to represent our Lord on this earth as a purifying agent and to shine forth the gospel of our Lord and Saviour Jesus Christ into the darkness of a world lost and dying in sin.

There is a story in God's Word describing the people's complaint to Elisha concerning water that was unfit to drink in the city of Jericho. Jericho is near the place where the Jordan River enters the Dead Sea. It may have been that the water from the Dead Sea had contaminated the ground waters at Jericho, making them bitter and unusable. Elisha responded to the people's request, and the waters were cured and became sweet for their use. The water at Jericho remains good to this day.

> *And the men of the city said unto Elisha, Behold, I pray thee, the situation of this city is pleasant, as my lord seeth: but the water is naught, and the ground barren. And he said, Bring me a new*

cruse, and put salt therein. And they brought it to him. And he went forth unto the spring of the waters, and cast the salt in there, and said, Thus saith the LORD, *I have healed these waters; there shall not be from thence any more death or barren land. So the waters were healed unto this day, according to the saying of Elisha which he spake. (2 Kings 2:19–22)*

Notice that the waters were contaminated and resulted in death and the ground being unable to produce any living things. The sin that permeates our society today is deadly as well. It destroys the life in which it abides and takes away the blessings of God from the soul engulfed in it.

Behold, all souls are mine; as the soul of the father, so also the soul of the son is mine: the soul that sinneth, it shall die. (Ezekiel 18:4)

The death that God speaks of here refers to the second death, which is eternal separation from God in a lake of burning fire for all eternity. What a horrible place to end up for those who reject God's plan of salvation through His Son's death, burial, and resurrection. God is not willing that any should perish but that all should come to repentance and be saved (2 Peter 3:9). It is left to each individual to make their decision for Christ or to reject Him and the forgiveness of sin that He freely offers to all who call upon His name.

It is God's desire that His children be the salt and light that those lost in sin need to find their way back to Him for the forgiveness of sin and healing of their souls. I believe that we can apply Elisha's story to our lives today. God's children are the new cruse, and the gospel message going forth from them is the healing salt to lead lost souls to the Saviour. We, as His children, must live in such a way that our testimony can be received by those around us. God cannot use a dirty vessel to send forth His Word. Jesus was emphasizing to His disciples on the mount the important task that lay ahead of them. They were to carry the gospel message to the world and teach them all the things that Jesus had commanded them, baptizing them in the name of the Father, and of the Son, and of the Holy Ghost (Matthew 28:18–20). That remains the commission of the New Testament church today and for every born-again believer to live in such a way that their lives are vessels fit for the Master's use.

There is a warning in God's Word concerning salt that has lost its savor. In other words, it must have the strength to make a difference for someone to realize that it is there. I like cold watermelon with a good sprinkling of salt on it. For me, the salt enhances the flavor of the melon. I can easily tell whether or not I have added salt to the watermelon. Jesus was teaching His disciples that their lives would be like that salt when they carried the gospel message forth to those lost in sin. Their lives must be pure and free from sin to allow their listeners to receive the gospel message and be saved. They must be able to sense the power of God in the lives of those presenting His Word to them.

Perhaps one of the saddest verses in the Bible is when Lot went out and tried to warn his family of the destruction to come, but because of his lifestyle, his testimony was not received by them.

> *And Lot went out, and spake unto his sons in law, which married his daughters, and said, Up, get you out of this place: for the LORD will destroy this city. But he seemed as one that mocked unto his sons in law. (Genesis 19:14)*

His seeking after fame and fortune had caused him to compromise his godly values, and the power of his testimony was lost to his family in their greatest hour of need. His married daughters and their husbands perished in the fire and brimstone that consumed that place, and his wife, who looked back, lost her life as well. His salt had lost its savor and was good for nothing. His backslidden, sinful life brought darkness to his life and those around him when the precious light of God should have been shining forth from him.

Don't, for a moment, think that this couldn't happen to us as well. For God's children to be salt and light to this world, we must live for our Lord and continually seek His face and His power in our lives. It is imperative that we resist the devil and his temptations and remain pure in our walk with the Lord.

> *Be ye not unequally yoked together with unbelievers: for what fellowship hath righteousness with unrighteousness? and what communion hath light with darkness? And what concord hath Christ with Belial? or what part hath he that believeth with an infidel? And what agreement hath the temple of God with idols? for ye are the temple of the living God; as God hath said, I will dwell in them, and walk in them; and I will be their God, and they shall be my people. Wherefore come out from among them, and be ye separate, saith the Lord, and touch not the unclean thing; and I will receive you, And will be a Father unto you, and ye shall be my sons and daughters, saith the Lord Almighty. (2 Corinthians 6:14–18)*

This is a powerful portion of scripture for God's children in today's world. With violence and immorality on every hand, we must separate ourselves from the sin that seeks to destroy our effectiveness for our Lord. We are the salt and light in our world today and represent our Heavenly Father to those around us. The above text asks us what agreement (concord) hath Christ with Belial (Satan)? Indeed, there is no agreement between Christ and the devil, and there should be no agreement between the children of God and sin.

We conclude this book with these thoughts: It is God's children who can and should make a difference in today's world. America's greatest need is for the born-again children of God to stand up, speak up, and be the salt and light that this sin-darkened world needs today. When Jesus was on earth, He said, "I am the light of the world." Now that He has gone back to His Father, He has left us here to be that light that shines into the sin-darkened lives of those around us. The light of the gospel sets men and women and boys and girls free.

Let your testimony shine forth today and every day for our Lord. Make a difference in the lives of others. I close this writing with a blessed promise from our Heavenly Father. America needs His healing touch today. He has promised to heal our land if we will humble ourselves before Him, pray, seek His face, and turn from our wicked ways. It is we, the children of God, who can make a difference for our nation in its greatest time of need. I encourage you to seek the Lord with all your mind, body, and soul and be that salt and light that He wants you to be.

> *If my people, which are called by my name, shall humble themselves, and pray, and seek my face, and turn from their wicked ways; then will I hear from heaven, and will forgive their sin, and will heal their land. (2 Chronicles 7:14)*

> *The LORD bless thee, and keep thee: The LORD make His face shine upon thee, and be gracious unto thee: The LORD lift up His countenance upon thee, and give thee peace. (Numbers 6:24–26)*

About the Author

Alton Lynn Cooper is an ordained minister and has served as a pastor to the Deaf at Capitol City Baptist Church in Holt, Michigan, for forty-five years. During this time, Alton served in prison ministry at Carson City Regional Correctional Facility in mid-Michigan for eleven years. His classes at the prison included both deaf and hearing prisoners, with many being saved and discipled in God's Word. Along with serving in ministry, Alton worked as a manufacturing manager in the automobile industry at General Motors Corporation for forty-one years. He is currently serving as a pastor emeritus at CCBC, supporting both deaf and hearing ministries throughout the church.

Alton and his wife, Dolly, have begun writing and publishing a number of Christian books to glorify God and encourage His children as they walk with Him. They desire to see many come to Jesus Christ and receive Him as their personal Lord and Saviour and for God's children to be strengthened in their faith.

Together, they have participated in mission trips and educational tours in Israel, Mexico, Honduras, England, Ireland, Scotland, Wales, Egypt, and Jordan, along with trips in the United States, working in vacation Bible schools and building projects at Bible colleges and youth camps.

Alton and Dolly have ten adult children, seven sons and three daughters, along with a host of grandchildren and great-grandchildren. They enjoy traveling and spending time with family and friends along the way while being salt and light to those with whom they come into contact.

God bless you and keep you in His care. May your pathway be brightened day by day as you walk in our Saviour's love.

BOOKS BY ALTON LYNN COOPER

The Grampa Hal children's series (color illustrated)

Grampa Hal Comes to Visit
Rooster for Rent
Hats with Headlights
The Fish That Wouldn't Stay Caught
The Frog That Wouldn't Hop
Flies That Don't Burn
Jeepers and Creepers
The Crazy Little Train That Goes in Circles

Tall Tales for Little People (ten illustrated short stories for children)

Full-length novels (Christian fiction)

Wellmington's Cove
The Long Dusty Road
The Bend in the River
On the Wings of Love
Caleb's Mountain

Christian discipling books

Godly Priorities for Christian Living (released under Alton Cooper)
Finding Peace and Joy in a Troubled World (released under Lynn Cooper)
Building Godly Relationships (released under Lynn Cooper)
The Coming Wars
Salt and Light

Samuel Garcia Private Eye Mystery Series

In the Dark of Night
The Case of the Vanishing Masterpieces
Gone without a Trace

Glory to God Publications LLC
Alton Lynn Cooper—Christian author / speaker
Dolly Jean Cooper—editing / illustrating/ technical support
Visit our website: gtgaltonlynncooper.com.

Their books are available through Christian Faith Publishing, Amazon, Barnes & Noble, BAM! (Books A Million), Ingram, Spring Arbor, Russell Books, iTunes, Indigo, McNally Robinson, Sword of the Lord Publications, Trilogy Publishing—Trinity Broadcasting Network (TBN), and in most Brick and Mortar bookstores.